HISTORY
OF
THANATOLOGY

Philosophical, Religious,
Psychological, and Sociological
Ideas Concerning Death
from Primitive Times
to the Present

Panos D. Bardis

UNIVERSITY
PRESS OF
AMERICA

To

Donna Jean,

Byron Galen,

and

Jason Dante,

Who have enabled me to dream of a
constellation of emeralds, a
forest of cypresses, and a garden
of acacias.

iii

"It would be natural to mention
all the different causes of death,
in order that the one real cause
of that man's death be mentioned
among them."

Lecretius, *De Rerum Natura*, VI.

"Now the goods of the present life
pass away, since life itself passes
away, which we naturally desire to
have, and would wish to hold
abidingly, for man naturally shrinks
from death."

Aquinas, *Summa Theologica*, I-II,5,3.

TABLE OF CONTENTS

PREFACE

In August 1979, I was invited to present a paper at the Conférence Internationale de Sociologie Religieuse in Venice, Italy.

My report gradually evolved into a comprehensive history of death, which resulted in the present book--an interdisciplinary and cross-cultural, as well as sociohistorical, study. Thus, this volume covers both East and West: China, India, Persia, Mesopotamia, ancient Egypt, the Greco-Roman world, Judaism, Christianity, Islam, and medieval and modern times. Most of the numerous definitions of death are included, and both theory and practice are stressed. No major discipline that has something to say about death is neglected.

It is obvious that in a parochial, ahistorical, materialistic, industrial, and hedonistic era, we must place greater emphasis on spiritual ideals, the meaning of life, the nature of death, and some of the contributions made in these areas by major cultures, both past and present. Besides, as Euripides said, "Who knows that what is called death is life, and life is death?" More systematic thinking about such issues makes our physical and nonphysical worlds more human and meaningful.

Of course, there are literally countless publications on death. These are of five main types:

1. Brief, impressionistic, and limited essays and articles.

2. Empirical studies each of which deals with a minute aspect of death.

3. A few monographs on specific topics.

4. A few fairly comprehensive textbooks.

5. A few bibliographies.

But there is no comprehensive, cross-cultural, interdisciplinary, and readably organized outline of the history of thanatology, including both ideas and practices. Although this is a formidable goal, I have attempted to achieve it as much as possible. Thus, this book can function as a reference work, a supplementary source, a counseling aid, and so on--it is hoped that the detailed index will be very helpful.

Consequently, the readership can include a variety of groups--since thanatology is now popular, even students in the natural sciences take college courses dealing with death. In other words, this history of the science of death is aimed at students (in high school and, especially, college), teachers in related fields (religion, philosophy, psychology, sociology, etc.), other professionals (ministers, social workers, physicians, counselors, and the like), and even intelligent laymen.

Panos D. Bardis, Ph.D., F.I.A.L.
Editor, Social Science
Professor of Sociology
The University of Toledo

CHAPTER ONE

INTRODUCTION

The purpose of the present book is to explain, evaluate, and synthesize the most important ideas, from primitive times to the present, regarding death.

The science dealing with death is known as thanatology (Greek thanatos, death, and logos, word or science). The complexity of this discipline is partly suggested by the following facts:

It seems that, when social integration is dominant and social values are accepted automatically, the awareness of death is limited. But when social disorganization is prevalent and individualism intensifies, the consciousness of death becomes stronger. The latter have occurred in Hellenistic times, during the early Renaissance, and in the 20th century. The study of death has also been more intensive and extensive during these three periods.

Such research, however, has usually been neglected by great philosophers. Baruch Spinoza (1632-1677), for instance, has only given us one single sentence on death, unlike men of letters, who have written much more concerning this subject. Perhaps, philosophers have been neglectful simply because they are not very interested in death. The modern English and American

1

analytic philosophers have even asserted that
the limited study of death proves that this
phenomenon cannot really be explored
philosophically. Two things explain their
attitude: first, their war on metaphysics;
and second, their belief that the social
sciences and psychology can study death much
better. Indeed, one of the major modern
steps in this direction was a symposium on
the psychology of death, which was included
in the 1956 American Psychological Association
Convention. At any rate, whenever
philosophers did study death, they emphasized
four basic issues:

1. The nature of death.

2. Knowledge of death.

3. Fear of death.

4. The social and psychological forces
affecting our knowledge of death.

As for the first of these four issues,
most religions have considered death, not as
a natural occurrence, but as a consequence of
a supernatural attack.

Another prevalent attitude throughout
history has been that birth control is much
less important than death control (except for
infanticide and child exposure, human
sacrifice, cannibalism, capital punishment,
and war). This explains why fertility rates
are decreasing more slowly than mortality
rates. Moreover, in high mortality societies
death threatens the entire community, which
results in wide cooperation aimed at the
solution of problems generated by death. In
low mortality cultures, however, death merely
threatens the personality system, thus being
a personal tragedy, namely, one involving
relatives and friends. Consequntly,

2

bereavement assumes a tremendous variety of forms.

The complexity of thanatology is further indicated by varying definitions of the individual. In rural Puerto Rico, for example, the child is regarded as an incomplete person, sinless, pure, and innocent. This means that, after death, he joins the angels, which explains why children's funerals are joyful affairs. Among the Arapaho Indians, however, the child is considered similar to adults and, like them, departs to the land of the spirits after death. His burial, therefore, is an adult ritual during which his parents slash themselves and engage in other forms of exceedingly emotional behavior.

Similarly, some societies have considered senilicide, or geronticide (the killing of the aged), perfectly acceptable. This may be accomplished through homicide or suicide-- either forced or voluntary. The reasons for geronticide are at least five:

1. Fear of an old person's superior knowledge, greater power, or higher social status.

2. The belief that he has already had a full life.

3. His limited economic productivity-- he feels and is considered useless.

4. Social isolation of the elderly.

5. The subsistence level of a society's economy--the climate is severe, life is rather nomadic, and the supply of food is inadequate.

But the Murngin of Australia consider old age a status symbol, their age statification being characterized by elaborate rites of passage. The highest stratum consists of the oldest members of that society.

Death by <u>suicide</u> is also a highly complex phenomenon, as varying definitions suggest. In his <u>Mohave Ethnopsychiatry and Suicide</u> (1961), George Devereux indicates that the Mohave think of the following events as forms of suicide:

1. Actual suicides.

2. Funeral suicides.

3. Vicarious suicides.

4. Stillbirths.

5. Infant deaths after abrupt weaning because of a new pregnancy.

6. Death of one or both twins before marriage or in childbirth.

7. Symbolic suicides in incestuous unions.

A special type of suicide is the <u>Samsonic</u> form, which is based on revenge against an enemy.

As for <u>burial</u>, only man buries the dead. The earliest evidence reveals that hygiene was not the reason for this, but that a primitive philosophy of life and death led to funerary ritualism. Paleolithic man, for instance, buried the corpse together with food, tools, and ornaments, which means that an afterlife was part of this primitive philosophy. Even Neanderthal man (50,000 B.C.) had similar beliefs and customs.

Additional problems are created when we

consider man's fear of death. Empirical research indicates that the lowest fear is found among true believers and nonbelievers in religion, while nominal believers experience the highest fear. Furthermore, man has usually defined death as being killed, not as a natural end of his life. For this reason, he has learned to kill instead of being killed--he has fought disease, increased longevity, transplanted organs, and is now beginning to create life; and he has invented destructive weapons for his protection, which intensifies man's fear of death. The same result is seen in the common belief that "Death will come to you, not to me," which generates additional armaments and, thus, a greater fear of death.

Such fear and other related emotions seem to follow a pattern in the case of a terminally ill person. Elisabeth Kübler-Ross has presented the following five stages in her famous book, On Death and Dying (1969):

1. Shock and denial ("Not me!").

2. Anger against physicians, nurses, his family, friends, and even God ("Why me?").

3. Bargaining for life, usually through prayer.

4. Depression (preparatory grief).

5. Acceptance.

Kübler-Ross admits that this sequence is not universal, and that a patient may move back and forth or go through more than one stage at the same time.

CHAPTER TWO

DEFINITION OF DEATH

But what is death?

Once more, the complexity of this subject is also revealed by our futile efforts to define it.

A common definition is that death is the absence of life. This assertion, however, is exceedingly naive, since it is negative, namely, it tells us what death is not, not what it is.

In general, since life has not always been explained naturalistically, death has often been described supernaturally. Some primitives, for instance, attribute it to gods or demons. Religion has referred to it as the departure of the soul from the body, or the destruction of the body-soul unity. More specifically, Christianity saw Adam's sin as the cause of death, while a modern philosopher, Martin Heidegger (Sein und Zeit, 1927), has averred that death is not a natural phenomenon.

In law, death has been defined in three main ways:

1. "Natural death" is "the cessation of life," or "the ceasing to exist," or a total stoppage of the circulation of the blood, and

7

a cessation of the animal and vital functions consequent thereon, such as respiration, pulsation, etc.

2. "Civil death" is the state of a person who, though possessing natural life, has lost all his civil rights, and as to them, is considered as dead.

3. "Violent death" is one caused or accelerated by the interference of human agency.

Another legal type, "presumptive death," refers to that which is presumed from proof of a long continued absence unheard from and unexplained, such absence usually lasting seven years.

From the physical point of view, there is a distinction between clinical death, which refers to the entire organism, and biological death, which covers individual organs. Since not all the components of the organism discontinue their function simultaneously and to the same extent, death has also been defined as a process. In other words, the line between life and death is always arbitrary, depending on our purpose and criteria.

Traditionally, clinical death has been regarded as the absence of the following: a heartbeat (therefore, lack of a peripheral pulse), breathing (thus, presence of bluing of the lips, mouth, and limbs), and certain eye reflexes. In addition, three other conditions make their appearance: algor mortis (the chill of death), rigor mortis (rigidity of skeletal muscles), and livor mortis (cutaneous purple-red spots on portions of the cadaver due to the settling of the blood). But most mammals have six essential parts, that is, the gastrointestinal,

8

excretory, respiratory, circulatory, nervous,
and supportive systems. And their damage
does not lead equally to death. For instance,
there is no death even when much of the bone
is lost or if a kidney stops functioning for
hours. But if the heart and lungs discontinue
their function even for a few minutes, death
may result. Now, however, this definition
becomes inadequate, since clinical death may
be prevented by means of pacemakers,
respirators, and the like. In fact, this is
even true of cases where the brain has stopped
functioning, namely, when cerebral death has
occurred.

Brain death, of course, which means
cessation of the brain processes, presents an
additional difficulty. This is the
philosophical mind-body problem, one of the
most controversial hypotheses dealing with it
being the "identity thesis," namely, that
brain processes and consciousness coincide.

Cellular death involves the cell, which,
as is well known, lives only when growth,
assimilation, and division occur. Nerve cells,
however, are never replaced, and replacement
does not present the same rate for all cells.
Besides, it is exceedingly difficult to
determine exactly when the homeostatic
mechanism of the cell undergoes irreversible
damage, that is, death. Then, the same kind
and degree of damage is not equally
destructive to all cells. Phosphorus, for
example, affects the peripheral cells of the
liver, and chloroform the central cells.
Hypoxia (lack of an adequate amount of
oxygen) does not damage all cells similarly.
A cell may rupture (cytolysis), or its nucleus
may shrink (pyknosis), fragment (karyorrhexis),
or rupture (karyolysis). Finally, electronic
microscopic inspection reveals cell damage
quite early, whereas light microscopic
inspection does so several hours later.

In general, cerebral and cardiorespiratory functions were considered interdependent in the past. Modern technology, however, has separated these functions, which now can continue independently. Of course, there are degrees of biological disintegration, some of the marginal states between life and death being artificial survival, coma vigil (delirious lethargy with open eyes and partial consciousness), coma depassé, persistent vegetative state, and irreversible coma. More specifically, a distinction has been made between <u>cardiac death</u> and <u>brain death</u>, the latter being subdivided by some authorities into <u>cerebral death</u> and <u>cortical death</u>. In brief, it seems more helpful to distinguish between cardiological and neurological criteria of death, while the traditional criteria have been of two types: three primary (respiration, cardiac pulse, and blood pressure) and one secondary (body temperature).

Finally, medical conferences during the late 1960's have stressed <u>irreversible coma</u> as a criterion of death. This refers to a permanently nonfunctioning brain, that is, a flat electroencephalographic recording, or absence of brain waves. These conferences have also emphasized a lack of spontaneous cephalic reflexes, muscular movements, and respiration. Later, the criterion of an agonal angiogram was added (diminished blood circulation). Unfortunately, these criteria are unsatisfactory in cases of hypothermia (body temperature below 90°F), or severe central nervous system depression due to a drug overdose. Besides, irreversibility cannot be determined objectively, for what was irreversible in the 19th century can now be reversed, and the 20th century's irreversible coma may be reversed in the 21st century.

10

CHAPTER THREE

THE EAST

The philosophical and religious ideas of the East concerning death have been dominated by two main principles:

1. Emphasis on meditations that make death less destructive and even creative.

2. The belief that ethics and medicine must be combined to increase longevity and generate harmony between man and the cosmos.

When East and West are compared, two chief differences emerge:

1. In the Orient, salvation is achieved through mysticism and contemplation, in the West, through active asceticism.

2. After death, Orientals believe, the deceased attains an impersonal and homogeneous oneness with the cosmos, whereas in the West there is a continuation of a distinct and personal self.

A. China

Since Chinese thinkers have emphasized human existence, an early death constitutes an anomaly that prevents full personal development. Furthermore, a young person's death produces an evil spirit that threatens the entire community. This explains why, throughout Chinese history, longevity has been valued. Accordingly, in ancient times, the Chinese mourned the death of a young person, but rejoiced when the deceased was over 70 years of age.

As for the nature of life and death, it was never examined thoroughly by Chinese philosophers. Confucius (557-479 B.C.) avoided the subject almost completely. In general, the ancients merely defined death as the dispersion of the body-soul system, the latter component usually being considered of two types, yang, or male principle, and yin, or female principle. Occasionally, a person might have more than two souls. In view of the prevailing familism, especially the concept of filial piety, it was further believed that the deceased became a sacred ancestor. Some mention of heaven and hell was also made. In addition, many philosophers, particularly the Taoists, asserted that, ultimately, the components of man would return into the Tao, that is, the cosmic origin of life (W. Soothill, The Three Religions of China, 1919).

Preparing a dying person included shaving his head, paring his nails, and placing him in a sitting position, thus facilitating the departure of the soul. To prevent the dead from harming the living, ancestral shrines were built containing tablets on which the names of one's ancestors were inscribed. The upper social classes constructed more tablets of this kind. Offerings were also made.

B. India

In the sixth century B.C., for the first time in human history, we encounter, in Indian Buddhism, the sophisticated doctrine that death means personal extinction--even Neanderthal man believed in life after death.

12

Of course, Buddhism and Hinduism are vast and complex, thus presenting a tremendous variety of concepts concerning death, some of which are as follows:

Dualism here implies that a person consists of a physical body, as well as of an immortal inner soul or self. The cyclical philosophy of reincarnation states that the soul is reborn into another human or animal body after death. Nirvana, or enlightenment, is achieved when the person has annihilated all desire to life in the material world. Reincarnation is the result of some primordial transgression, while the soul's conduct in this world determines the nature of its afterlife.

It is often stated that Buddhism has emphasized life negation. This, however, is not entirely true, which explains why longevity has been valued tremendously. Mahayana (Great Vehicle), for example, has stressed a long life through prayer. The highest point of this belief is found in Japan, where the ascetics of the Shingon sect pursued longevity through self-mummification. After death, many sages asserted, one may be reborn in heaven or in hell, depending on how virtuous one's life and last thought have been, the last thought being the result of one's deeds and beliefs during life (E. Thomas, The Life of Buddha as Legend and History, 1927).

In the ancient Vedic Hymns, worldly existence was also stressed, which led to rituals and prayers aimed at longevity (H. Griswold, The Religion of the Rig-Veda, 1923). In fact, a century was often considered synonymous with immortality. That is why later Hindu mythology pursued rejuvenation in four ways:

1. Intervention by a saint.

13

2. Exchanging life with another human.

3. Residing in a sacred place.

4. Listening to the holy writings.

The early Vedas taught that those who live righteously, namely, according to rta (universal cosmic law), will continue a similar life after death. A popular belief throughout Indian history has been that, if a person's mind is dominated by virtuous thoughts at the time of death; or, if his ashes are purified by the waters of the Ganges; or, if he dies in a sacred place, especially Benares; then, after death, he will have a heavenly rebirth. Medieval Hinduism included the doctrine that a wicked life leads to hell. In general, many sages throughout the history of India considered death good, since, when it occurs, the soul becomes free of the cycle of metempsychosis (A. Keith, Buddhist Philosophy in India and Ceylon, 1923).

In another sphere, death (marana) is regarded as the last of the 12 links (nidanas) that bind man to the Wheel of Life. Thus, death is the abandonment of the body (rupa), which now dissolves. Death also is one of the four recollections (the other three being body, breathing, peace), which are sometimes added to the six basic recollections (anussati), namely, recollection of the Buddha, his doctrine, his community, morality, detachment, and the heavenly sphere. The monk who recollects death, every morning and every evening, contemplates the countless dangers of life that invite death constantly, and thus subdues his evil tendencies, which lead to eons of suffering if they are still present at death (Anguttara-Nikaya, VIII).

Mara, the personification of death,

14

actually means "death agent," or "killer," and is similar to the Western Devil. Buddha himself was often tempted by Mara, who tried to prevent him from attaining enlightenment. During Buddha's ministry, the demon sometimes approached the great religious leader in the form of a human or animal (Mara-Samyutta). In the less advanced writings of Buddhism, Mara is the lord of the lowest of the three planes of existence, that is, Kama (Sensual World). In more sophisticated scriptures, he becomes the symbol of everything evil, impersonal, and impermanent. In general, Mara represents a transition from popular superstitions about discarnate evil spirits to more abstract psychological and moral doctrines regarding the human condition (E. Windisch, Mara und Buddha, 1895).

After a person's death, there was a funeral procession to the place of cremation. First went a man carrying a firebrand from the hearth of the deceased. The mourners walked around the bier carrying the corpse. On the way, a goat was sacrificed and, when the procession arrived, an elaborate cremation ceremony occurred during which the widow crouched by the funeral pyre (in older times, she was cremated alive--suttee custom). A short time later, the remains of the deceased were scattered in a sacred river. The straddha, a monthly festival involving offerings to three generations of dead ancestors, was aimed at keeping their spirits from harming the living.

Chinese Buddhism includes 10 hells similar to Dante's Purgatorio, where the dead pay for their transgressions before returning to this world. And Tibetan Buddhism describes the next world as a dreadful place, which explains why the dead need guidance and advice, given to them by Bardo Thodol (The Book of the Dead).

15

C. Persia

When Zoroastrianism, Persia's main
religion, which was founded by Zoroaster or
Zarathustra (sixth century B.C.), moved from
eastern Iran to Media, the local priests,
known as Magi, added to the new faith their
own ritual of exposing the dead. Thus, on
the high dakhmas (towers of silence), the
corpse was devoured by birds of prey. Such
exposure was based on the belief that burial
or cremation would pollute the earth.

To achieve eternal life after death,
according to Zoroastrianism, one did not have
to adopt asceticism or life negation. A moral
life was sufficient. This meant that, in the
perpetual struggle between good and evil, or
Ahura Mazda and Ahriman, man must side with
the former deity.

Then, at the time of death, his good and
evil deeds will be judged. If he has been
virtuous, he will be sent to heaven; if
wicked, to hell. If, on the other hand, his
good and evil deeds are balanced, he will
find himself on an intermediate plane, where
pain and pleasure are combined.

Finally, when Ahura Mazda defeats
Ahriman, this intermediate world will come to
an end and all souls will be purified by
fire. A new earth and a new heaven will then
be created--an eternal kingdom of peace,
happiness, and righteousness. As for
Ahriman, he will return to the realm of
perpetual darkness (M. Dhalla, History of
Zoroastrianism, 1938).

D. Mesopotamia

In Babylonian mythology, the realm of
the dead is also grim, ghastly, and dreadful.
A famous myth involving Ishtar reveals much

16

concerning Mesopotamian thanatology.

Ishtar was the Babylonian goddess of fertility and the evening manifestation of the planet Venus--Frazer identified her with the Esther of the Old Testament. According to a tablet kept in the British Museum, Ishtar descended into Aralu, the Babylonian Hades, in search of her husband Tammuz, an Assyrian-Babylonian god (Ezekiel 8:14) who was sometimes called Adonis (from Adon, Lord). Aralu kept the dead in frightening gloom forever and ever--in the Gilgamesh Epic there is a superior realm for those killed in battle, now resting on couches and drinking clear water. The queen of Aralu was Allatu, a solar goddess and the female counterpart of Allah in the pre-Islamic pantheon (Bruno Meissner, Babylonien und Assyrien, 1925).

When Ishtar found the Seven Gates of the underworld locked, she threatened to destroy them, to release the dead, and to devour the living. Allatu thus permitted Ishtar to enter, leaving one of her garments and jewels at each gate. She finally arrived naked in the realm of the dead, whose bread is dust, whose food is mud, who see not the light, who dwell in darkness, and who are clothed like birds in apparel of feathers. Her task accomplished, Ishtar returned to earth after having recovered her garments and ornaments at each of the Seven Gates.

Ishtar's grim descent and ritual nakedness symbolize the attributes of life which the dead gradually lose while entering the Babylonian Hades. As for their macabre living conditions in this region, it is not surprising that it was customary in ancient Babylon to provide food and drink for the spirits of the dead in order to prevent them from wandering about in search of nourishment.

In brief, the Mesopotamian divinities often helped mortals in illness and calamity, but never in death, since, when the gods created man, they assigned death to him, but they kept life in their own hands. And when death finally came, a man's status in the underworld depended on the way in which he died and was buried, on the number of children that he left behind, and on the sacrifices offered on his grave. His evil deeds were not punished and his good deeds were not rewarded after death (Edouard Dhorme, La Religion Assyro-Babylonienne, 1910).

CHAPTER FOUR

ANCIENT EGYPT

The ancient Egyptians, perhaps more than any other people, devoted considerable attention both to death and to life after death (E. Budge, Osiris, 1961; The Book of the Dead). Their dream was to die after the age of 110 years and to have a good burial. The prevalent belief was that death is an unhappy event that brings tears and sorrow. It snatches a man from his home and throws him on a desert sand-dune. For this reason, he will never return to the earth or see the sun again. Although two important divinities, Sekhmet, the bloodthirsty leonine goddess known as the Lady of the Messengers of Death, and Bastet, a cat goddess, were associated with death, there was no Egyptian god that personified death. Still, death was described as a ferocious plunderer: "I was a young child when I was carried off by violence....I was suddenly torn away in my youth....I had a crowd of friends but no one could defend me....My father, my mother, prayed to death, my brothers were prostrated" (The Book of the Dead). Thus, the ancient Egyptian thought of death continually, while at the same time enjoying his life: "Follow your heart and the pleasures which you desire....The day of lamentation will come even for you and weeping will not bring back a man from the other world....Behold, no one can take his possessions with him and no one has ever come back after he has gone there" (ibid.).

19

The main philosophy dominating Egyptian thanatology was that defining human nature as a psychophysical organism, a well-integrated existence, all of whose parts, including the body, are essential. For this reason, the body must be preserved for future reanimation through the highly elaborate ritual of mummification (G. McHargue, Mummies, Chapter 3). This ritual, which was an imitation of the death and resurrection of Osiris, the death god whose myth constitutes Egypt's greatest contribution to religion, included the "Opening of the Mouth" of the mummy to facilitate life through nourishment.

More specifically, as Herodotus (484-424 B.C.) tells us, to enable the spirit to find the weakest component of the human being, namely, the body, embalming proceeded as follows: first, a metal hook was used to remove the brain. This process was completed by means of encephalic drainage (dissolving the remainder with drugs). Then, with an Ethiopian stone, the side was cut and the viscera were removed (evisceration). After filling the abdomen with palm oil, spices, and aromatic powders, the body was sewn up. Thus, mainly the less corruptible skin, cartilages, and bones remained. These were dehydrated by immersion of the corpse in salt of natron for 70 days (the priests had observed that Sirius vanished below the horizon for 70 days, and modern chemists have proved that salt of natron will dehydrate a mummy entirely). Hundreds of yards of fine gauze and bandages, protective amulets, stone eyes, and more aromatic substances completed mummification. At each stage, which symbolized a step in the death and resurrection of Osiris, the priests recited passages from the sacred texts--for instance: "You will live again, you will live again forever! Behold, you are young again forever!" (Herodotus, Histories, II, 85-90).

20

A prehistoric belief, which was the oldest Egyptian doctrine concerning death, was that life after death continues almost unaltered. Although it was slightly modified later on, this principle was never abandoned, which explains the "embryo" position of the corpse in the tomb and the abundance of food and drink buried with it. To make life in the tomb more prosperous, the walls were decorated with detailed scenes of harvest, vintage, fishing, hunting, and the like. A magic formula, it was believed, could easily bring this bucolic and rustic panorama to life. Much of the labor involved in this area would be performed by the ushabtis (answerers), small statues placed in the tomb. The dead man himself would spend his day in his grave, occasionally visiting familiar places of the upper world. At night, he would follow the sun on its subterranean journey and stop in the fields of Osiris. And at dawn, he would hasten to the coolness of his tomb. The dream of the ancient Egyptian, therefore, was an adequate tomb containing a table laden with food and drink that could be renewed periodically. In other words, the dead depended on the living more than the living feared the dead; for a second death in the tomb was final, hideous, and dreadful (E. Budge, Egyptian Magic, 1901; The Gods of the Egyptians, 1904).

In early times, when kings were wealthier and more powerful, their funerary provisions also fed their dead subjects. But when royal authority declined and the middle classes began to appear (after the IV Dynasty, or 2600 B.C.), personal funerary foundations came into existence that paid a priest to maintain a dead man's tomb (A. Erman, Die Religion der Aegypter, 1934; S. Mercer, Horus, 1942).

A typical funeral in Thebes consisted of

21

four steps:

1. Mourning and praying in the dead man's house.

2. Carrying the deceased and some of his possessions to the Nile.

3. Journey on the river by funerary barques, including a boat transporting the bier which supported the coffin and the mummy, with two lamenting women standing on either side (these symbolized Isis, the sister and wife of Osiris, and Nephtys, another sister of Osiris, who were known as the Weeping Sisters).

4. Gathering of the cortege on the west bank, procession to the necropolis, and burial.

The first coffins, used mainly for the sake of dignity, appeared in the beginning of the third millennium B.C. In later times, however, when elaborate sarcophagi were added, coffins in human shape became part of the funeral ritual.

The Egyptians also introduced sepulchral iconography. The portrait of King Djoser of the III Dynasty (2686-2613 B.C.), for instance, appeared in the Step Pyramid together with his name and accomplishments, for both commemorative and magic purposes.

After the funeral, it was further customary to perform dances that would vitalize the dead person.

The first known statement dealing with the journey of a deceased person is found in the Pyramid Texts (2375-2200 B.C.). The description mentions countless dangers, an evil ferryman, dreadful monsters, lakes of fire, and so on. A dead pharaoh, on the other hand, ascends a ladder to join the gods, or flies to the solar boat of the sun god Ra, or visits the stars around the pole.

Such preoccupation with death is finally indicated by the vast and complex funerary texts, which are of five main types:

1. Independent magic formulae.

2. The cosmographic books of the New Kingdom or Second Theban Empire (1567-1085 B.C.).

3. Ritual liturgies of the dead.

4. The handbooks of the Late Period (715-330 B.C.).

5. Rituals of the dead gods.

An unusual doctrine for those times was the moral judgment of the dead in Tuat, the Egyptian nether world. Here, the dead man's heart was weighed against Maat (Truth), while Osiris, the god of the dead, watched. If he were found to be wicked, the dead man was devoured by the monstrous Am-mut (Eater of the Dead).

CHAPTER FIVE

ANCIENT GREECE

Homer (8th century B.C.) referred to
Thanatos, the Greek god of death, as the
brother of Sleep. About half a century later,
Hesiod added that "Night gave birth...to
Thanatos" (Theogony, 211-212). The greatest
Greek artists represented Thanatos as a
sleeping youth or as a young man carrying an
inverted torch.

Hades was the dreadful kingdom of the
dead. Its entrance was guarded by Cerberus,
a three-headed dog with snakes growing from
its neck and a tail that was a dragon. He
always let the souls enter through the gate,
but devoured all those who attempted to return
to the upper world. To pacify this hideous
monster, the ancient Greeks sent him honey
cakes with the corpses. The ruler of this
kingdom was also called Hades (Unseen), or,
euphemistically, Pluto (Giver of Wealth).
Since no mortal expected any favors from him,
the Greeks never dedicated a temple to Pluto,
and the artists seldom created his image.
Pluto's queen was Persephone, and the realm's
three judges were Minos, Aeacus, and
Rhadamanthys. The River Acheron, or perhaps
Styx, was the barrier between life and death.
Three other infernal rivers were the Cocytus,
Lethe, and Phlegethon. Charon, the demonic
boatman, ferried the dead across the Acheron
and collected the coin placed in the mouth of
the corpse by the bereaved family. The souls

went to one of Hades's three regions:

1. __Tartarus__, the most miserable section, where wicked mortals, such as Tantalus and Sisyphus, were punished.

2. __The Plains of Asphodel__, an intermediate place.

3. The pleasanter __Elysium__, or __Elysian Fields__, also known as the __Islands of the Blessed__, which was the home of those who had found favor with the gods (Achilles, Diomedes, Menelaus, etc.). These led full and happy lives here and, according to later philosophers, returned to life on earth after 1,000 years, or rose to the sun, the pure light and bliss of the gods.

After death, the body was placed in a sepulcher, which was often cut in the rock, sometimes in groups. The corpse usually lay on a stone couch. An interesting example is the famous Harpy Monument in the British Museum, but the supreme representative of the temple-tomb type was the Mausoleum of Halicarnassus, one of the Seven Wonders of the World. Also celebrated are the beehive tombs of Mycenae, such as the Treasury of Atreus. Some corpses were buried in graves similar to ours. In Attica, for instance, the dead were originally interred in their homes, but later on away from the city and usually by the side of a road. The gravestones were of eight main types: round columns, rectangular slabs, stelae, shrine-shaped stones, huge rectangular stone blocks, marble vases, square or round receptacles for the ashes, and sarcophagi. If the body were cremated, the remains might be placed in clay coffins or urns. Various objects, often valuable ones, were also buried in the tomb. In classical Athens, __sepulchral iconography__, which reached its noblest heights

26

in that city at that time, included three
elements:

1. A brief inscription--usually the
name and parentage of the deceased and,
occasionally, the word "Farewell."

2. The restrained grief of the living.

3. The image of the dead person doing
something familiar for the last time.

The sarcophagus (flesh-eater), which was
adorned with funerary scenes from mythology,
was made of limestone from Assos in Troas.
According to Pliny (23-79 A.D.), "corpses
buried in it are consumed within 40 days,
except for the teeth" (Naturalis Historiae,
xxxvi, 27)--this must have been a fissile
limestone.

In Homeric times, patriotism led to the
belief that eternal recognition, fame, and
glory awaited those who died as heroic
warriors. According to Homer's Iliad, the
body of such a hero was washed and perfumed
and then mourned by men and women, most of
whom were hired for this purpose. The corpse,
which was never embalmed, was consumed by the
funeral pyre together with several living
human beings--12 Trojans were thus sacrificed
on the pyre of Patroclus. The deceased was
also honored with games, the victors receiving
generous prizes. Finally, the funeral closed
with a banquet (Iliad, XXIII, 35-225).

In the Greek polis, it was also considered
noble to die for the common good. But by now,
as in the case of classical Athens, new laws
put an end to expensive and extravagant
funerals even for prominent citizens. Although
mourning continued, funerals further became
shorter, mainly for hygienic reasons. The
stela that was placed on the grave during or

27

after the funeral was both a tomb indicator
and a symbolic boundary between life and death,
which explains why it played an important part
in various strange cults. In addition, Athens
had a special ceremony, the Anthesteria, which
commemorated the dead. On that day, the keres,
or souls, left the tombs and returned to their
homes where they were provided with food. At
sundown, the living sent the souls away with
these tragic words: "Out, keres, the
Anthesteria is ended!"

Orphism (600 B.C.), a Greek mystical cult
founded by Orpheus, the Thracian musician,
poet, and prophet of the Dionysian religion,
was one of the first Hellenic systems to deal
with death profoundly and philosophically.
Its dualism described a physical body and an
immortal inner soul or self. The soul's
incarnation in the body was the result of some
primordial transgression, but its conduct in
this world would determine the nature of its
afterlife. In other words, Orphism included
a cyclical philosophy of reincarnation,
namely, the soul's rebirth into another human
or animal body. Because the next world was
horrible and frightful, and the dead man's
journey to it exceedingly dangerous, the
Orphists guided the soul by means of
instructions written on gold laminae that were
placed in the grave.

The pre-Socratic philosophers of Greece
stressed both continuity and change, saw
harmony between man and physis (nature), and
conceived of human life as part of a cosmic
order. Of these, Phythagoras of Samos (572-
497 B.C.) was the only one to speculate about
death seriously. One of his doctrines was
that of the transmigration of the soul, which
occurs exclusively within the animate world.
Heraclitus of Ephesus (540-475 B.C.) spoke of
eternal cosmic change, which excludes the
Logos, the immutable law of change itself.

28

Parmenides of Elea (born 515 B.C.) believed
in perpetual stability, while Herodotus of
Halicarnassus (484-424 B.C.), the so-called
father of history, wrote about the death of
man and of entire civilizations. His studies
convinced him that there is nothing evil in
such extinction. If fact, he believed that
death may be superior to life, and that it is
the gods' best gift to man.

The ideas of Socrates (469-399 B.C.)
regarding death are mainly found in Plato's
(427-347 B.C.) Apology, Crito, and Phaedo.
Fewer, but also important, comments on this
subject are made in the Republic, Gorgias,
and Symposium. These ideas are as follows:

1. The true philosopher is cheerful
when death is near.

2. After death he achieves the greatest
good in the world.

3. Death means separation of body and
soul.

4. The soul exists freely and
independently.

Unlike Plato, who employed mathematical
models that led to the concept of the Ideas,
Aristotle (384-322 B.C.), whose father was a
physician, studied biology and used biological
models that influenced his thinking about the
ethical aspects of death. His early ideas,
according to the Eudemian Ethics, were that
the soul is more important than the body, that
the body is the soul's prison, and that the
soul goes through Pythagorean transmigrations.
Later, however, in his De Anima, transmigration
was rejected and the soul was defined as the
entelechy (the condition of a thing whose
essence is fully realized, or actuality as
distinguished from potentiality) of the body--

as hearing is the entelechy of the ear. A
special form of death, infanticide, was
justified, according to Aristotle: "as for
the exposure and rearing of children born, let
there be a law that no defective infant shall
be reared" (Politics, 1335b).

After the Hellenic period, which ended
with the death of Aristotle (322 B.C.) and was
succeeded by the Hellenistic stage,
philosophers, unlike the pre-Socratics,
Socrates, Plato, and Aristotle, studied death
both extensively and intensively. The
Epicureans and Stoics were particularly
interested in this subject.

Of these, Epicurus (341-270 B.C.) was the
first in the Mediterranean world to state the
sophisticated doctrine that death is personal
extinction--even Neanderthal man believed in
an afterlife. Influenced by the atomistic
physics of Democritus of Abdera (460-360
B.C.), he rejected immortality, since the soul
is merely a constellation of the finest
material atoms which, at death, disintegrates.
Thus, like Lucretius (98-54 B.C.), Epicurus
spoke of ataraxia, or freedom from anxiety and
worry, and of death as a blessing that was to
be welcomed. To free man from fear of the
gods and of the ultimate extinction of the
individual, he also gave us one of the first
solutions to this problem. Such fear, he
reasoned, is based on the twofold belief that
death is painful and that this pain continues
in the afterlife, both of which are false.
First of all, death is entirely painless and,
in view of the atomistic theory, immortality
is impossible, since the soul is destroyed at
death. In his famous Letter to Menoeceus,
Epicurus asserts: "Therefore, the most
horrible of all evils, death, is nothing to
us, for when we exist, death is not present;
but when death is present, then we are not.
So it is not present either for the living or

30

for the dead, since for the former it does not
exist, and the latter do not exist" (Diogenes
Laertius, Epicurus, 125). Many philosophical
and religious systems, however, do include
immortality. Besides, fear of death may be
based, not on pain, but on man's unwillingness
to accept nonexistence. Miguel de Unamuno
(1864-1936), for example, used to say that,
when he was a child, the most macabre pictures
of hell never frightened him, but the idea of
nothingness did.

Zeno of Cyprus (335-265 B.C.), the founder
of Stoicism in Athens, stressed physics. His
philosophy was that man must live according to
nature, namely, according to reason, which
means that we should never oppose unavoidable
evils, including death. His disciples in
Rome, Seneca (55 B.C. - 41 A.D.), Epictetus
(55-135 A.D.), and Marcus Aurelius (121-169
A.D.), preached aequanimitas (peace of mind)
and apatheia (indifference). Seneca added
that the best way to diminish the fear of
death is thinking of it constantly. Epictetus
conceived of death as a necessary thing and
even as a solution when we face unavoidable
evils. Suicide thus becomes an assertion of
freedom, as in the case of Seneca. Marcus
Aurelius also dealt with death frequently in
his Meditations. In general, the Stoics
averred that the only proper goal of
philosophy is preparation for death.

CHAPTER SIX

ANCIENT ROME

The Etruscans, who influenced the Romans considerably, began to construct tombs mainly during the sixth century B.C. These were hewn out of the rock and were usually subterranean. A famous example is the temple-tomb of Norchia. The tombs of Etruria were similar to the houses of the living--there were paintings and various household objects, as well as stone couches for the corpses. The funeral ended with games that included some shedding of blood, which was of a sacrificial nature.

The Romans usually placed their tombs by the side of a road, as in the cases of the celebrated pyramid of Gaius Cestius and the tomb of Caecilia Metella on the Appian Way. Of course, the most spectacular such structure in Rome is the Mausoleum of Hadrian. The Street of Tombs in Pompeii is also well known. According to Cicero (106-43 B.C.), "a dead man, says the law of the Twelve Tables, must not be buried or burned within the city. I believe that the latter is on account of danger of fire. But the addition of the words 'or burned' indicates that a body which is cremated is not considered buried, but only one which is inhumed" (De Legibus, 58). The cases of Gaius

Fabricius, the Vestal Virgins, and the emperors, who were buried inside Rome, were exceptional. Another kind of tomb was the columbarium (pigeon house), a subterranean structure with many niches for the urns containing the ashes of the dead. Over the niches were marble tablets for the names of the occupants. Such tombs were usually built either by prominent Romans for their servants, slaves, and freedmen (e.g., Emperor Augustus, and Empress Livia, on the Appian Way, for more than 3,000 dead) or by occupational and religious societies for their members, who contributed an initial payment and an annual subscription. As for Rome's sepulchral iconography, its portraits were chiefly commemorative, not of magical value.

The funerary procession included ancestral masks and the custom of the os resectum, namely, the burying of a finger joint after the rest of the body had been cremated, which seems to have been a vestige of earlier inhumation. The funeral banquet that took place in the tomb chapel recalls the Bavarian Leichennudeln (corpse cakes) and the Welsh "sin eating."

Of Rome's thinkers, the Stoic Seneca (55 B.C. - 41 A.D.) taught that we must not fear death. The true philosopher is especially too dignified to be intimidated by such extinction, and philosophical contemplation will easily liberate him from similar concerns. More specifically, the best solution to this problem is to think of death constantly, stressing the fact that we are part of nature and, therefore, must accept our destiny. Seneca gave us two famous analogies:

First, life is a part in a play and we must not question the limits imposed by the dramatist.

34

Second, life is a banquet and we must not rebel against its time boundaries.

It has already been mentioned that Marcus Aurelius (121-169 A.D.) discusses death in the 12 books of his Meditations quite frequently. To the emperor, death is as natural as birth, since development inevitably leads to an end. Death, therefore, must never be feared.

CHAPTER SEVEN

THE OLD TESTAMENT AND JUDAISM

The book of Genesis contains two theories concerning immortality:

1. Since burial unites the body with the soil, the first theory derives Adam's name from haadamah (earth). Thus, like a potter, God made man from earth, which means that, as in the case of animals, man's mortality was part of the original plan of creation: "And the Lord God formed man of the dust of the ground, and breathed into his nostrils the breath of life; and man became a living soul....And out of the ground the Lord God formed every beast of the field, and every fowl of the air" (2:7,19).

2. Originally, God created man as an immortal being, but disobedience led to his mortality: "But of the tree of the knowledge of good and evil, thou shalt not eat of it: for in the day that thou eatest thereof thou shalt surely die" (2:17).

The soul resulting from such creation was less definite than those found in Greece and Christianity. According to the Hebrews, the human body merely includes ruah or nefesh, which is found in the breath or in the blood, and which creates life. Death means the loss of this force. Since a diminished life may continue to center on the skeleton, the Hebrews had a great deal of respect for tombs: "I will not turn away the punishment thereof; because he burned the bones of the king of Edom into lime" (Amos 2:1).

The immortality of the soul was also vague and seems to have been mainly collective, not individual, the emphasis being on property continuity and on having a good name and many descendants, especially sons: "neither let the eunuch say, Behold, I am a dry tree. For thus saith the Lord unto the eunuchs that keep my sabbaths....Even unto them will I give in mine house and within my walls a place and a name better than of sons and of daughters: I will give them an everlasting name, that shall not be cut off" (Isaiah 56:3-5); and "The memory of the just is blessed: but the name of the wicked shall rot" (Proverbs 10:7).

Although the spirit was considered important, biological life was also valuable, since it had been created by God: "Thou sendest forth thy spirit, they are created: and thou renewest the face of the earth" (Psalms 104:30). Even the killing of an animal without a proper ritual was regarded as murder: "What man soever there be of the house of Israel, that killeth an ox, or lamb, or goat, in the camp, or that killeth it out of the camp...blood shall be imputed unto that man" (Leviticus 17:3-4). This emphasis on biological life, which inspired respect even for the dead body, explains why Orthodox Jews have often condemned cremation and autopsies.

Death itself is not really stressed in the Old Testament, the prevailing attitude being that of Ecclesiastes: "a time to be born, and a time to die" (3:2). It is an

38

inevitable natural phenomenon: "And, behold, this day I am going the way of all the earth...all are come to pass unto you, and not one thing hath failed thereof" (Joshua 23:14).

As for the meaning of death, at least seven definitions are given in the Old Testament:

1. Complete biological destruction.

2. A physical, psychological, or social deficiency: "The Lord killeth, and maketh alive: he bringeth down to the grave, and bringeth up" (I Samuel 2:6).

3. The return to the former natural state: "Then shall the dust return to the earth as it was: and the spirit shall return unto God who gave it" (Ecclesiastes 12:7).

4. A form of sleep: "I will make them drunken, that they may rejoice, and sleep a perpetual sleep, and not wake" (Jeremiah 51:39).

5. A state in which God is not praised: "For in death there is no remembrance of thee: in the grave who shall give thee thanks"? (Psalms 6:5).

6. A state in which God is not seen: "I shall not see the Lord, even the Lord, in the land of the living" (Isaiah 38:11).

7. A force opposing God's cosmic harmony: "It shall devour the strength of his skin: even the firstborn of death shall devour his strength" (Job 18:13).

Moreover, in old age, death is accepted calmly: "Then Abraham gave up the ghost, and died in a good old age, an old man, and full of years; and was gathered to his people" (Genesis 25:8). But a premature death due to wicked behavior is dreadful: "fools die for want of wisdom" (Proverbs 10:21).

Death may even present the following advantages:

First, the brevity of life leads to the pursuit of understanding: "So teach us to number our days, that we may apply our hearts unto wisdom" (Psalms 90:12).

Second, death ends our suffering: "The small and great are there; and the servant is free from his master" (Job 3:19).

Third, it shortens the wicked man's conduct: "And it repented the Lord that he had made man on the earth, and it grieved him at his heart. And the Lord said, I will destroy man whom I have created from the face of the earth" (Genesis 6:6-7).

Fourth, the death of one generation elevates the next: "And the Lord's anger was kindled against Israel, and he made them wander in the wilderness forty years, until all the generation, that had done evil in the sight of the Lord, was consumed. And, behold, ye are risen up in your fathers' stead" (Numbers 32:13-14).

Fifth, death makes man stress the present: "A time to love, and a time to hate; a time of war, and a time of peace" (Ecclesiastes 3:8).

Inhumation, which was almost universal, was justified in terms of Adam's origin: "for dust thou art, and unto dust shalt thou return" (Genesis 3:19). The body, however, was almost

never embalmed and, because Canaan has many
caves, such places were frequently used as
tombs. Immediate burial was also common in
order to avoid unpleasant odors and to insure
ritual cleanness: "This is the law, when a
man dieth in a tent: all that come into the
tent, and all that is in the tent, shall be
unclean seven days" (Numbers 19:14).

The Hebrews' Sheol was a vague place
where the rephaim (souls) continued a partial
existence after death. Although a medium did
contact the ghost of Samuel (11th century
B.C.), the so-called last of the judges and
first of the prophets after Moses ("Then said
Saul unto his servants, Seek me a woman that
hath a familiar spirit, that I may go to her,
and inquire of her. And his servants said to
him, Behold, there is a woman that hath a
familiar spirit at Endor"--I Samuel 28:7),
the Hebrews condemned such communication:
"Thou shalt not suffer a witch to live"
(Exodus 22:18). Besides, they believed that
the dead do not really affect the living much:
"their love, and their hatred, and their envy,
is now perished; neither have they any more a
portion for ever in any thing that is done
under the sun" (Ecclesiastes 9:6). Enoch
further describes a place similar to Dante's
Purgatorio (I Enoch 22:9-13), but this was
during the first and second centuries B.C.
Finally, it seems that the evil souls were
sent to eternal torment and the righteous
ones to everlasting good: "And many of them
that sleep in the dust of the earth shall
awake, some to everlasting life, and some to
shame and everlasting contempt" (Daniel 12:2).

In Talmudic times, the Jews believed in
tehiat hametim (resurrection of the dead),
death being the gate to olam haba (the world
to come). On the Day of Judgment, the
righteous went to heaven and the wicked to

hell, or Gehenna. Euthanasia was rejected
even for the terminally ill, who were
considered complete living persons (Shabbat,
151a). Abortion was against the law and
suicide was condemned--a person who committed
suicide was neither mourned nor given a
funeral.

As for the etiology of death, there were
two dominant theories, both of which included
the belief that thinking of death is
conducive to righteous living:

1. Death is the result of biological
cyclical evolution.

2. Death is due to sin, which is
universal, death itself thus also being
universal.

Post-Talmudic Judaism developed two
schools of thought, The Zohar (The Book of
Splendor) and the Scholasticism of Moses
Maimonides (1135-1204).

The Zohar accepted gilgul, or
transmigration of the soul (either for
punishment or for the sake of completing
one's unfinished work on earth), and
described heaven and hell in detail. It also
mentioned dibbuk (attachment) and ibbur
(impregnation) of a person with another soul,
a condition that may be terminated through
exorcism. In other words, the dead are
capable of helping or harming the living.
Accordingly, one must not visit cemeteries
at certain times and the mirrors in a dead
man's house must be covered. Such customs
have been especially common among the
Hasideans of East Europe.

Maimonides taught that the soul is
complex, intelligence being its highest

42

component. This part of the soul is immortal, since it is able to contemplate immortal entities, chiefly God's nature. Therefore, the understanding of eternal truths leads to immortality, which is a perpetual and blissful vision of God by the soul.

Among modern Jews, the more liberal ones have emphasized the immortality of the soul at the expense of the bodily resurrection of the dead. Gehenna (hell) and Eden (paradise) have also been rejected. The first important Jewish thinker in modern times was Moses Mendelssohn (1729-1786), who brilliantly defended the concept of an immortal soul (Phaedon, 1767).

CHAPTER EIGHT

THE NEW TESTAMENT AND CHRISTIANITY

Because of Hellenistic influences, Christianity dealt with death much more extensively than the Old Testament did. But its emphasis on eternal life prevented Western philosophy from studying death systematically. An important Christian concept is that of dualism, namely, soul versus body, or eternal-spiritual world versus temporal-material world. Man, having an immortal soul, is in the middle of these two poles, the ideas of Easter-resurrection giving him hope. Thus, as in the hymn Dies Irae, death means a metamorphosis, not the end of life. The ultimate goal in this system is salvation, that is, eternal life with God. That is why, according to the Gospel of John, biological death is less important than one's deeds, and those who accept the teaching of Jesus become immortal: "And whosoever liveth and believeth in me shall never die" (11:26). Indeed, the New Testament explains that Jesus has conquered death: "Death is swallowed up in victory. O death, where is thy sting? O grave, where is thy victory?" (I Corinthians 15:54-55).

The New Testament defines death in at least five ways:

1. The end of natural life: "But Jesus said unto him, follow me; and let the dead bury their dead" (Matthew 8:22).

2. The departure of the soul from the physical body: "For I am now ready to be offered, and the time of my departure is at hand" (II Timothy 4:6).

3. The laying aside of the body: "For we know that if our earthly house of this tabernacle were dissolved, we have a building of God, an house not made with hands, eternal in the heavens" (II Corinthians 5:1).

4. A form of sleep: "Our friend Lazarus sleepeth; but I go, that I may awake him out of sleep" (John 11:11).

5. Complete separation from God, which is the second death: "Blessed and holy is he that hath part in the first resurrection: on such the second death hath no power....And death and hell were cast into the lake of fire. This is the second death" (Revelation 20:6,14).

As for the etiology of death, two main theories are presented:

First, death is the result of sin: "That as sin hath reigned unto death, even so might grace reign through righteousness" (Romans 5:21).

Second, death is caused by the spiritual night of God's absence from one's life: "To give light to them that sit in darkness and in the shadow of death" (Luke 1:79).

In New Testament times, burial almost always consisted in inhumation, embalmment was exceedingly uncommon, and the typical tomb was a cave. The body was wrapped in clean linen ("And when Joseph had taken the body, he wrapped it in a clean linen cloth"--Matthew 27:59), anointed with spices and ointments ("And they returned, and prepared spices and

46

ointments"--Luke 23:56), and buried
immediately in order to avoid unpleasant
odors: "and the young men came in, and found
her dead, and, carrying her forth, buried her
by her husband" (Acts 5:10). Coffins were
never used and the funeral (this word does
not occur in the Bible) was not elaborate.
Burial in sarcophagi with beautiful
iconographic illustrations began in the fourth
and fifth centuries.

In medieval times, the Catholic Church
adopted a funeral based on the belief in
purgatory. This ceremony included black
vestments, black candles, and the tolling of
church bells, and consisted of five main
stages:

1. A cortege of mourners and clergy
carried the corpse to the church, while psalms
were sung and incense was used for
purification.

2. The coffin was deposited in the
church and covered with a black pall. Then
followed the Office of the Dead, the
participants constantly repeating: "Eternal
rest grant unto him, O Lord: and let perpetual
light shine upon him."

3. The Requiem Mass came next.

4. The Absolution of the deceased
included perfume, incense, and holy water for
the coffin.

5. The burial of the body, with the
appropriate prayers, took place in consecrated
ground.

In modern times, the Second Vatican
Council (1962-1965) introduced white vestments
and prayers of joy and hope.

After death, God will raise the physical body again and judge every man's deeds. Then, the righteous will enjoy everlasting bliss in heaven: "For the Lamb which is in the midst of the throne shall feed them, and shall lead them unto living fountains of waters: and God shall wipe away all tears from their eyes" (Revelation 7:17). The wicked, however, will undergo perpetual punishment in hell: "But he that shall blaspheme against the Holy Ghost hath never forgiveness, but is in danger of eternal damnation" (Mark 3:29).

One of the greatest Christian thinkers, Saint Paul, made the first profound statement regarding resurrection. His use of the term soma, however, meant neither flesh nor spirit, but personality, ego, identity, Gestalt. He also theologized death, which, according to him, results from man's original sin: "by one man's disobedience many were made sinners" (Romans 5:19). But death was conquered by Jesus and resurrection now leads to a newness of life: "Christ was raised up from the dead by the glory of the Father, even so we also should walk in newness of life" (6:4). Death, despite its ephemeral biological victory, has lost its power, and those who believe in Jesus may now become immortal: "For this corruptible must put on incorruption, and this mortal must put on immortality" (I Corinthians 15:53).

The Apocryphal New Testament speaks both of immortality and of an active existence on the part of the soul. This is especially true of The Vision of Paul, which influenced Dante and generated the later belief that the soul often returns to the body to praise or scold it, depending on the state of the soul. The famous dialogues between body and soul concerning moral principles were also inspired by this book.

Later Christian thinkers contributed many

ideas to thanatology.

Saint Irenaeus (130-200 A.D.), the martyr
and bishop of Lyons in Gaul who wrote Against
Heresies, believed that the soul is immortal
but inactive after death. Its residence is
an invisible place where the soul is waiting
for the day of the Last Judgment (Against
Heresies, V, 31).

Saint Gregory (330-395 A.D.), the
Cappadocian Church Father who became bishop of
Nyssa, wrote De Anima et Resurrectione. In
this brilliant treatise, he defined the soul
as man's immortal or divine component, adding
that the body and soul cannot be separated
completely. After death, Gregory said, the
soul merely waits for the day of resurrection,
which means the reunion of the body and soul.

Saint Augustine (354-430 A.D.), one of
the greatest Latin Church Fathers and the
author of De Civitate Dei, defined death as
man's punishment for his sins. Concerning the
fear of death, he asserted that only divine
grace can liberate us from it.

Pope Gregory the Great (540-604 A.D.),
whose name was given to the Gregorian chant,
believed that death is the separation of the
soul from the body, and that their reunion
will take place at resurrection. Moreover,
the soul may go through purgation. As for
visions of life after death, which some
persons have, they are indicative of sanctity
that the truly virtuous achieve as soon as
death occurs.

Saint Anselm (1033-1109 A.D.), the
archbishop of Canterbury who became famous
for his ontological argument for the existence
of God, wrote the celebrated Cur Deus Homo?
on the atonement in 1097. This theory of

penitential discipline dealt with penances imposed by the Church. If a person died before completing such penances, he could continue them as an active soul between death and the moment of resurrection on Judgment Day. If no penances were necessary, or if the imposed penances were completed, the soul would enjoy a blissful existence after death. The soul, of course, was judged as soon as it left the body.

Saint Thomas Aquinas (1226-1274 A.D.), the greatest Schoolman of the Middle Ages and author of Summa Theologica, also believed in such rewards and punishments for the human soul after death.

Among modern Christians, Martin Luther (1483-1546) and John Calvin (1509-1564) rejected purgatory. Both of them, however, were basically medieval thinkers who placed great emphasis on the immortality of the soul and the period between death and resurrection. Later on, Catholicism stressed neo-Thomism, while Protestantism adopted a neo-orthodoxy based on the teachings of the reformers.

CHAPTER NINE

ISLAM

Ideas and customs pertaining to death
(maut) have not been uniform throughout the
Moslem world. In general, the time of death
is fixed for every living creature in advance:
"If God were to punish men for their wrong-
doing, He would not leave on the earth a single
living creature; but He respites them until a
stated time; and when their time comes they
cannot delay it an hour, nor can they hasten
it" (Koran, XVI, 63). The Angel of Death
(Malaku 'l-Maut), somewhat similar to the Greek
Charon, is the spirit that causes death and
takes the soul (XXXII,11). According to
Mohammed, this event does not inspire fear
among Moslems, since, "When death comes near
a believer, then God gives him a spirit of
resignation, and so it is that there is nothing
which a believer likes so much as death."

The Koran contains two words for soul,
ruh (XVII, 87) and nafs (III, 24). Moslem
theologians consider these terms synonymous,
but philosophers distinguish between them as
follows: nafs is similar to the Greek psyche
and means life or soul, whereas ruh, like the
Greek pneuma, stands for spirit. Man thus
consists of three parts, jism (body), nafs
(soul), and ruh (spirit). This division does
not occur in the Koran, but it is found in the
New Testament: "I pray God your whole spirit
and soul and body be preserved blameless unto
the coming of our Lord Jesus Christ" (I
Thessalonians 5:23).

A dying man must be placed facing Mecca, the birthplace of Mohammed and the most holy city of Islam. Sharbat, a mixture of water and sugar, or holy water from the Zamzam well in Mecca, is then poured into his mouth in order to facilitate the exit of the vital spark. To prevent an unpleasant appearance, the mouth is closed and tied. The two great toes are also tied with cloth together to keep the legs from spreading apart. The body is further washed and perfumed thoroughly.

The burial (janazah means both bier and funeral service) is speedy, since, as the Prophet himself observed, a prolonged funeral would inconvenience the family of the deceased.

Although the Koran and the Traditions of Islam do not specifically prohibit cremation, the burning of a dead body is strictly forbidden. This is because the Moslem faith does not permit the burning of a living person, as well as because it is believed that a dead body is as conscious of pain as a living one. Mohammed himself taught: "Punish not with God's punishment. Verily it is not fit for anyone to punish with fire but God" (Mishkat, XIV, 5); and "The breaking of the bones of a corpse is the same as doing it in life" (V, 6).

The funeral service must not take place in the cemetery, which is considered too unclean for such a sacred rite, but in the mosque or in an open space. The officiating person usually is the family imam. During this service, the people say to the relatives of the deceased, "It is the decree of God," and the chief mourner answers, "I am pleased with the will of God."

Although the use of coffins is not forbidden, the corpse is seldom placed in a coffin. The open bier is usually carried by

four relatives or friends, and it is regarded
as a great honor to perform this task.

Unlike the Christian funeral procession,
which is very slow, the Moslem one is quite
speedy. The reason for this is Mohammed's own
statement that, if the deceased was wicked,
then the living must get rid of him as soon
as possible, but if he was righteous, he must
be quickly carried to his place of eternal
peace. Moreover, the procession must go on
foot, since Mohammed said: "Have you no
shame? God's angels go on foot and you go
upon the backs of quadrupeds?" The angels,
of course, go before the corpse, which explains
why all mortals are expected to walk behind
the deceased. In addition, the mourners
should refrain from wearing bright clothes.

The corpse is placed in the grave (qabr)
on its back, with the head to the north and
the feet to the south, and facing toward
Mecca. When filling the grave with earth,
some Moslems pray as follows, which recalls
the Genesis account of man's creation: "From
it have We created you, and unto it will We
return you. And out of it will We bring you
forth the second time" (Koran, XX, 57). The
use of unburnt bricks in the construction of
the tomb was allowed by Mohammed, but mortar
and inscriptions were forbidden (Mishkat, V,
6). Many Moslems, however, particularly
important ones, have had spectacular tombs of
mortar, stone, marble, and the like. The
sepulcher of Taimur (died 1405 A.D.) in
Samarkand is a miniature chapel of remarkable
beauty and elegance. The octagonal mausoleum
of Suleiman the Magnificent (1490-1566 A.D.)
in Constantinople, made of marble of various
colors, is more famous. The most celebrated
Moslem tomb, of course, is the white marble
Taj Mahal in Agra, India, built by Emperor
Shah Jahan between 1630-1652 over the grave

of his favorite wife, Urjummad Banu Begum, who was known as Mumtaz-i-Mahal (The Exalted One of the Palace).

An unusual episode that occurs on the night after burial is the Azabu'l-qabr (Chastisement of the Tomb). Munkar and Nakir, two black angels with blue eyes, visit the deceased to give him an examination concerning his faith. This explains why the roof of the tomb is constructed in such fashion that the dead person is able to sit up, and why an expert, the fiki, instructs the deceased immediately after the funeral on the right answers. If he replies correctly, his grave expands miraculously, a light appears, and he sleeps in peace. But if he proves to be an infidel, "The wicked will be struck with a rod, and they will roar out, and their cries will be heard by all animals that may be near the grave excepting man and the genii" (Mishkat, I, 5). There is nothing symbolic about such punishment. According to Moslem tradition, Mohammed was once riding a mule through a graveyard and both actually heard the shrieks and groans of the dead. The Prophet said: "If I were not afraid that you would leave off burying, I would ask God to give you the power of hearing what I hear." This punishment continues until Judgment Day.

Islam's Purgatory (Barzakh), somewhat similar to the Greek Hades, is the grave itself, or a partition between life and Judgment Day. Every dead person resides there until the day of resurrection, the believers resting peacefully and the infidels suffering perpetual pain and agony. Mohammed said: "There are appointed for the grave of the unbeliever ninety-nine serpents to bite him until the Day of Resurrection" (Mishkat, I, 5). The Koran adds: "And say, My Lord, I seek refuge with Thee from the incitings of

the devils, and I seek refuge with Thee from
their presence. Until when death comes to any
one of them, he says, My Lord! send me back,
if haply I may do right in that which I have
left. Not so! A mere word that he speaks!
But behind them there is Purgatory, until the
day when they shall be raised. And when the
trumpet shall be blown, there shall be no
relation between them on that day, nor shall
they beg of each other then" (XXIII, 99).

The Koran also includes many beautiful
descriptions of al-yaumu l'akhir (the last
day, Judgment Day, and the like), one of the
most famous being the following: "When the
sun shall be folded up, And when the stars
shall fall, And when the mountains shall be
set in motion, And when the she-camels shall
be abandoned, And when the wild beasts shall
be gathered together, And when the seas shall
boil, And when souls shall be paired with
their bodies (LXXXI, 1-7). When this day
comes, God will raise the physical body, judge
each person's deeds, and reward the righteous
with everlasting bliss in heaven and the
wicked with eternal punishment in hell. The
Prophet said: "The doors of the celestial
regions shall not be opened for them, nor
shall they enter into paradise till a camel
passes through the eye of a needle."

CHAPTER TEN

THE MIDDLE AGES

Medieval thanatology has already been discussed under Christianity and Islam. Therefore, only a few additional comments will be made in this chapter.

First of all, it must be remembered that medieval Europe was influenced considerably by Plato, Aristotle, and the Scholastics. The influence of the ancients on this period was intensified by the philosophy and science presented by two giants.

One was Avicenna (980-1037 A.D.), the Arab Moslem physician, statesman, and philosopher who was born in Bokhara, Persia. Known as the "third Aristotle," he influenced Christian Europe through his more than 100 books, especially his brilliant commentaries on Aristotle (384-322 B.C.). His 18-volume encyclopedia covered mathematics, physics, logic, and metaphysics. The Soul was a poem published in 1030. Although he adopted Aristotle's dualism, he modified it to make cause and effect simultaneous, which means that God and his creation are coeternal. Also influential was his famous doctrine that the universal exists ante res in God, in rebus as the universal aspect of the particulars, and post res in man's mind through abstraction. Thus, the so-called "revival of Aristotle" in medieval Europe began with the Latin translation of Avicenna's works by Dominicus Gundissalinus in collaboration with Avendeath ibn Daud.

The other thinker was Averroes (1126-1198 A.D.), a Spanish Arab born in Cordova, then a Moorish city. He was a mathematician, physician, theologian, philosopher, judge, and statesman. Although he was sufficiently profound to be known as "The Philosopher," his more common epithet was "The Commentator"-- Dante referred to him as the author of "il gran commento." This is because his supreme achievement was to write a vast and brilliant commentary on Aristotle, which influenced medieval Catholic philosophers considerably-- even Thomas Aquinas (1226-1274 A.D.) imitated Averroes's analysis (M. Horten, Die Metaphysik des Averroes, 1912). Averroes's own chief work, On the Unification of Philosophy and Religion (1160), was exceedingly influential. One of his doctrines was that God created the universe ex nihilo and the two have been coeternal--Thomas Aquinas objected that this assertion cannot be proved or disproved philosophically, and that the answer to this question is a matter of faith. Averroes also believed that there is one eternal truth, which we can comprehend in two ways: through philosophy, namely, natural knowledge, and through the Koran, that is, revelation. His theory of the "double truth" is more famous. This means that a proposition may be philosophically true but theologically false and vice versa. Thomas also rejected Averroes's belief in the unity of the intellect, that is, the doctrine that there is one intellect common to all humans. According to Thomas this doctrine is based on an inadequate definition of the person and denies personal immortality. Nevertheless, several comments by Aristotle himself, who became familiar to the medieval world chiefly through Averroes, seem to support the Arab philosopher's viewpoint. Finally, Averroes contended that the human soul is closely related to the brain and dies with it. But man also has Reason, which is immortal. It is this Reason that, when sufficiently cultivated, enables man to unite with the eternal and universal Active Reason.

Under the influence of such science and philosophy, the medieval world was constantly preoccupied with sin and salvation.

Sin, which Saint Augustine (354-430 A.D.) defined as any thought, word or deed against God's law, gradually underwent countless formal distinctions (material, formal, actual, habitual, mortal, venial, and so forth). Early Christian theology merely emphasized the New Testament definition of sin, which included the following elements:

1. The belief that the roots of sin lie in human character.

2. Paul's doctrine that sin, which is universal, is a violation of the natural law which is written in man's conscience.

3. Saint James's assertion that sin has its origin in the human will, and that each man is personaly responsible for his own transgressions.

4. John's emphasis on man's rejection of Christ and the judgment that follows.

In the feudal society of the eighth and ninth centuries, the new penitential system was accompanied by a rather external philosophy of sin. Thus, each sin was to be followed by a specific quantity of penance. With Saint Anselm (1033-1109 A.D.), however, sin was

personalized again. Moreover, the development
of confessional practice gradually generated
a major part of Saint Thomas's moral theology.

Salvation from sin has usually meant the
liberation of the soul from the bonds of sin
and its consequences and the attainment of the
everlasting vision of God in Heaven, not
merely by way of reward, but as the achievement
of man's proper end.

A rather unusual feature of thanatology
during this period was involved in burial.
This was the practice of burying the parts of
one and the same corpse in different places.
One of the most famous cases was that of
William the Conqueror (1027-1087 A.D.), whose
heart was buried in Rouen Cathedral, his
entrails in the Church of Chalus, and his body
in Saint-Étienne, Caen.

Also unusual was Ars Moriendi (The Art of
Dying), perhaps written in the late Middle
Ages by the Dominican Order of Southern
Germany. By 1475, these short treatises on
death, hundreds of copies of which still
survive, had appeared in Latin and seven
vernaculars. There are two versions, a short
one, which is a summary of the long one, and
a long version, which consists of six parts:

1. Sayings on death from various
Christian authors.

2. Advice to a dying person.

3. Questions leading to salvation.

4. Ways of imitating Christ's death.

5. Suggestions to relatives, friends,
and others present at the time of death.

6. Prayers

An important section of The Art of Dying
is the "Psychomachia," a war between good and
bad angels for the possession of the dying
man's soul. Moriens (the dying man) chooses
between five virtues (faith, humility,
detachment, hope, and love) and five vices,
which are the exact opposites of the five
virtues. One of the chief teachings in these
treatises is that we must not make Moriens
optimistic about recovering, since death,
which is not to be opposed, is the beginning
of a new life. Also included is advice by
Pope Innocent III (1160-1216 A.D.) that the
dying patient must not be given any medical
aid before his soul recovers. This recalls
Plato's similar theory, which is as follows:
"you must not treat the body without the
soul....For all things were sprung from the
soul, both the evil ones and the good ones in
the body and in the whole man....And the soul
must be treated with certain charms; and these
charms are good words....Do not allow anyone
to convince you that you should treat his head
with this medicine, who has not first offered
the soul to be treated by you with the charm.
Because now, he said, an error is being
committed against mankind, that is, certain
doctors attempt only one method of treatment
instead of combining mental and physical
health" (Charmides, 156e-157b). In John's
Gospel, Jesus also says to the man whose
physical infirmity he had cured: "sin no
more, lest a worse thing come unto thee"
(5:14).

As for reward and punishment after death,
in an illustration accompanying Ars Moriendi,
a demon whispers to Moriens: "Infernus factus
est" ("Hell has been prepared"). Such scenes
recall the dance macabre--perhaps both this
infernal dance and Ars Moriendi were partly
inspired by the Great Plague of 1348 A.D. But
there is a difference between the two: the

61

dance macabre causes fear and horror, whereas Ars Moriendi suggests a dignified death, thus being less necrophiliac than it has often been thought.

CHAPTER ELEVEN

MODERN TIMES

The modern era has been dominated by secularism, naturalism, and science, while Bacon and Descartes may be regarded as the two fathers of modern philosophy. Of course, this new spirit has influenced recent thanatology. Some of the major schools and movements, and their attitudes toward death, are as follows:

Darwinism has viewed physical decline because of age and illness coldly and unsympathetically. Persons in this state are considered inferior and parasitical. Thus, death is a desirable end.

The **existentialists** of the late 19th century were the first philosophers to treat death extensively, intensively, and seriously. One of their contributions to the problem of the fear of death was their novel solution, which consisted in stressing the goal of social immortality at the expense of personal immortality. Existentialists further asserted that human happiness is impossible, and that we must accept death by facing it constantly. If we do, then and only then are we able to enjoy whatever life has to offer to us. This, of course, is no consolation to man, since existentialists do not believe in a providential order of nature. Death thus becomes absurd.

The Spanish Fascism of the 1930's, as in the case of every other ideological conflict, considered its viewpoint synonymous with life, whereas its enemies constituted a negative force to be eliminated by death. In fact, its slogan was: "Long live death!"

By 1942, the Nazis had formulated their so-called "final solution." That was a combination of racism and genocide aimed at "racial health." Of course, the Nazi euphemism for such genocide was "euthanasia"!

In the communist world, including the Soviet Union, the solution to the problem of the fear of death is twofold, namely, hard work and identification with the Communist Party.

Let us now consider some of the greatest modern thinkers who have speculated about death.

Leonardo da Vinci (1452-1519), the great Italian inventor, military engineer, anatomist, and painter, believed that a happy day ends in happy sleep. Similarly, a happy life ends in a happy death. In other words, the answer to those who fear the end of life is that they should pursue happiness, since unhappiness is conducive to thinking of death fearfully. Of course, Christianity would present two arguments against Leonardo's advice: first, a happy life results from conquering the fear of death, which means that happiness is not the solution to the problem, but the outcome of the solution; and second, complete happiness is not possible in this life.

Michel de Montaigne (1533-1592), the great French philosophical essayist, was skeptical about the possibility of knowledge and suggested that we return to revelation and

64

nature. His celebrated Essays (1580-1588) include an important one on death, "To Philosophize Is to Learn How to Die." Here Montaigne advises us: "If we have learned how to live properly and calmly, we will know how to die in the same manner."

Francis Bacon (1561-1626), the English philosopher who became Lord Chancellor and wrote the first philosophical treatise in English (The Advancement of Learning, 1605), stressed science and opposed Aristotelian-Scholastic logic. His own inductive logic, the so-called Baconian method, included four steps: empirical observation, analysis of the resulting data, inference leading to hypotheses, and testing of hypotheses by means of additonal observation and experimentation (Novum Organum, 1620). Bacon's main concern about death was man's fear of the end of life, which fear we must make every possible effort to conquer.

René Descartes (1596-1650), the French philosopher who became one of the founders of modern epistemology and introduced the use of mathematics in speculative disciplines, stated two "self-evident" truths. One was the thinking self, for, as Descartes said, "Cogito, ergo sum" ("I think, therefore I am"). The other was God's existence, which he "proved" mathematically: the existence of a divine being is evident by the idea of such an existence, as in the case of a triangle, in which the equality of the three angles to 180° is evident by the idea of a triangle (Discours de la Méthode; Principia Philosophiae). Like Francis Bacon, he opposed the fear of death, which man must attempt to conquer. Unlike Bacon, however, Descartes stressed the survival of the soul through the Cartesian dualism of the res cogitans (mind) and the res extensa (body).

Of course, the "mind-body" problem is still with us.

The mathematical method of Descartes was also employed by Baruch Spinoza (1632-1677), the Jewish philosopher and optical lens grinder of Amsterdam whose Ethics (1677) actually is a treatise on metaphysics. Spinoza's one and only short sentence on death is as follows: "A free man thinks of nothing less than of death, and his wisdom is not a meditation upon death but upon life" (Ethics, IV, 67). Since he never explained the meaning of this statement, we can only speculate that, to him, the rational man loses his fear of death by simply concentrating on life instead of thinking of death--François de La Rochefoucauld (1613-1680), the French author of maxims and memoirs, considered this method easy, since man cannot look directly at death, in the same way that he is unable to stare at the sun. Spinoza's solution is based on his psychological principle that a stronger emotion conquers a weaker one, emotional balance thus leading to a virtuous ethical life, while uncontrolled emotions generate moral disintegration. To him, the most powerful emotion is "amor intellectualis Dei" ("intellectual love of God"), which frees the soul from corrupting passions and disturbing emotions (Ethics; De Intellectus Emendatione, 1677). Spinoza's argument, however, seems weak for at least two reasons:

First, many fears are involuntary--we simply cannot tell a man not to think of death without explaining to him how this can be achieved.

Second, on the contrary, the Stoics and the existentialists would assert that man loses his fear of death exactly by thinking of the end of life.

Gottfried Wilhelm von Leibniz (1646-1716), the greatest thinker of 17th century Germany, rejected Cartesian mechanism and combined religion and science. An early father of modern symbolic logic, he invented a universal scientific language consisting of symbols. In the universe he saw beauty united with mathematical order and spoke of monads, genuine atoms existing metaphysically, which are the vital elements of the cosmos, and which are governed by a preestablished harmony created by God (Discourse on Metaphysics, 1686; New System of Nature, 1695). Leibniz believed in the immortality of the soul, as well as in "absolute death," in which all perception ceases entirely. As an optimistic philosopher, he added that animate beings never perish completely, since God always conserves our person.

François Marie Arouet de Voltaire (1694-1778), the French social critic, essayist, playwright, novelist, and historian, was a rationalist who opposed religion. Man, according to Voltaire, is able to control social change simply by following genuine ethics, that is, ethics stressing secular science and rejecting religious principles (Treatise on Metaphysics, 1734; Discourse on Man, 1737). In his famous Dictionnaire Philosophique (1764), he made the following statement about death: "The human species is the only one which knows that it will die, and it knows this through experience." This, of course, is true and, even if some other species do have such knowledge, it must be exceedingly rudimentary.

David Hume (1711-1776), the Scottish thinker who was a great philosopher of skepticism, thought of the human mind exclusively as a series of ideas or sensations (A Treatise on Human Nature, 1737-1739).

His skepticism influenced his treatment of ethics and religion, to which he attributed natural, not supernatural, origins, and which he saw resulting merely from man's social customs and mental habits. His "Essay on Suicide" includes three main ideas:

1. Death by suicide is not a sin, since God has given us the ability to facilitate survival through medicine, artificial shelters, and the like.

2. Suicide is not in any way an offense against society, since misery gives a man the right to kill himself.

3. This form of death does not constitute a transgression against the self, either, since man's very choice of suicide proves that such destruction is better than living.

Hume's ideas influenced Germany's Immanuel Kant (1724-1804), one of the greatest philosophers of all time, who taught metaphysics and logic at the University of Königsberg. Kant became famous as the philosopher of transcendental idealism and asserted that, although we cannot know things in themselves, we are capable of knowing things as phenomena. Morals and social life, he believed, would be impossible without certain transcendental concepts, or metaphysical entities, such as God, soul, immortality, and the like. He thus accepted, a priori, man's freedom, namely, the idea that man's will is autonomous and free. His well-known kategorischer Imperativ (categorical imperative) states: "Act on maxims which can at the same time have for their object themselves as universal laws of nature." Death by suicide Kant considered an offense against one's duty to oneself and all duty in general, as well as against world morality

(Grundlegung zur Metaphysik der Sitten, 1785).

Marie Jean Condorcet (1743-1794), who
committed suicide in prison after supporting
the French Revolution, was a rationalist. He
wrote on human progress, his conviction being
that such improvement results from scientific
advancements (Esquisse d'un Tableau Historique
des Progrès de l'Esprit Humain, 1795). This
mathematician, political theorist, historian,
and social reformer averred that happiness
prevents man from thinking about death
fearfully. Unhappiness, however, is conducive
to the opposite.

Johann Wolfgang von Goethe (1749-1832),
the German dramatist and poet, regarded death
as nature's way of creating new life--"stirb
und werde" ("die and live again"). "It is
entirely impossible," he also said, "for a
thinking being to think of its own nonexistence,
of the termination of its thinking and life,"
which he considered a convincing argument for
immortality. But Goethe did not say whether
prenatal nonexistence is unimaginable.

Georg Wilhelm Friedrich Hegel (1770-
1831), another German philosopher who taught
at the Universities of Jena, Heidelberg, and
Berlin, is known for his dialectic (thesis,
antithesis, synthesis), a method which he
applied to history (Wissenschaft der Logik,
1812-1816). The living individual, Hegel said,
is a particular person. Death unites the
individual with cosmic matter, bodily
corruption rendering him indistinguishable
from abstract being.

Arthur Schopenhauer (1788-1860), the
German philosopher of pessimism who was
influenced by Kant's critical idealism,
conceived of the world as blind will. Man's
own finite will is also blind and constitutes

69

the Cosmic Will's manifestation (Die Welt als Wille und Vorstellung, 1818). Life, according to Schopenhauer, who was the first great philosopher to deal with death in detail, is dominated by pain and the solution to this problem is indifference facilitated by the awareness of death. His Romantic view, which the existentialists have usually accepted, was that death is "the muse of philosophy."

The so-called father of sociology, Auguste Comte (1798-1857), was a French philosopher who developed the system of positivism and identified three stages in the history of humanity: theological, metaphysical, and positive (Cours de Philosophie Positive, 1830-1842). Comte believed that human society consists of both its living and dead members.

August Weismann (1834-1914), the German biologist who developed his own ideas about evolution, formulated the theory of the "continuity of the germ plasm," namely, that life is continuous and potentially immortal. Samuel Butler, who opposed Darwinism, thus said: "A hen is only an egg's way of producing another egg." Weismann predicted the function of chromosomes and disproved Lamarck's notions by cutting the tails off 1,592 mice over 22 generations, and discovering that the offspring always had normal tails. On the basis of these ideas, he concluded that nature merely leads every organism to its death after reproduction has been completed.

Another German biologist and philosopher, Ernst Heinrich Haeckel (1834-1919), added to the theory of evolution his own concept of "material monism," namely, that the entire cosmos is one material substance (The Riddle of the Universe, 1904). Therefore, he opposed all revealed religions and their notions concerning God. He thus suggested that human

70

beings who are inferior and useless must be
poisoned by the hundreds of thousands.

The greatest German antipositivist was
Friedrich Nietzsche (1844-1900), a
psychological philosopher who admired
Zoroastrianism and the ancient Greek
civilization. Nietzsche taught that the
absolute value of all life is the will to
power, that is, the instinct to achieve
authority and excellence--the Nazis distorted
this principle perilously (Also sprach
Zarathustra, 1883-1884); Jenseits von Gut und
Böse, 1886; Zur Genealogie der Moral, 1887).
He also attacked the Romantic idea that death
is "the muse of philosophy," asserting that
a sound philosophy of life should consider
human mortality, but not death itself.
Moreover, the "will to die" can be neutralized
by the concept of "eternal recurrence" and
life affirmation through art. His Übermensch
will not be surprised by death, since he is
always aware of this state, happily thinking
of death as the natural end of life. Although
Nietzsche rejected the altruistic ethics of
positivism and averred that death can be
chosen by the individual egoistically, he
himself preferred a long life of misery and
excruciating pain to suicide.

Sigmund Freud (1856-1939), during World
War I, stated that the consciousness of death
is superficial, since the unconscious accepts
its immortality. Later, however, he
inconsistently spoke of an unconscious death
wish. But, in general, the founder of the
psychoanalytic school stressed life (Eros) at
the expense of the death instinct (Thanatos).
He further theorized that ignoring death
deprives life of a sense of urgency, adding
that, without the awareness of death, life
would be a Platonic romance. But "our own
death is unimaginable," although we can easily

conceive of another person's death. "Whenever we make the attempt to imagine our death...we really survive as spectators," which means that it really is not our own death, since we still exist as observers. Obviously, here Freud confused the content of a thought with its occurrence.

Émile Durkheim (1858-1917), the French sociologist who applied positivism to sociology (neopositivism), considered the sacrifice of oneself for society as man's chief ethical goal. Still, although he believed that the rights of the individual are less important than setting an example for the collectivity, he condemned suicide. He further advocated altruism through solidarity with others, especially within the family. His famous typology of suicide involves three forms:

1. Altruistic suicide is death for the benefit of the collectivity, which is similar to the political ideology of the ancient Greek polis, where it was considered noble to die for the common good.

2. Egoistic suicide is due to strong social norms, weak group integration, and intense feelings of personal responsibility, failure, and guilt.

3. Anomic or normless suicide results from personal or social disorganization (Suicide, 1897).

Henri Bergson (1859-1941), the French-Jewish philosopher who won the Nobel Prize in 1927, substituted "duration" for mechanistic "time," and believed in unlimited progress for mankind through an original life force, or élan vital, which is transmitted from one generation of organisms to the next. It is

72

this vital force that, as it permeates all reality, supports the belief in immortality (Matière et Mémoire, 1896; Les Deux Sources de la Morale et de la Religion, 1932).

Bertrand Russell (1872-1970), the English mathematical philosopher, made two major contributions: first, he developed new ideas in modern logic, which he considered a general theory of science, not a philosophical function; and second, he strove to unify the methods of science and philosophy (Introduction to Mathematical Philosophy, 1918; Inquiry into Meaning and Truth, 1940). His famous statement about death was: "When I die, I shall rot and nothing of my ego will survive." Russell also believed that happiness keeps us from thinking about death fearfully, while unhappiness and misery are conducive to the opposite.

Max Scheler (1874-1928), the German phenomenologist, asserted that death is an immanent structure of human consciousness (Philosophical World View, 1929). This is unlike Voltaire's belief, who based such awareness on experience.

Martin Heidegger (1889-1976), the German thinker who taught philosophy at the University of Freiburg and practically founded modern existentialism, rejected conventional philosophical concepts (body, soul, and so forth) and introduced Angst (Dread) and Sorge (Concern). In this system of existential phenomenology, Concern means the structure of consciousness, while Dread is the feeling of being on the verge of nonexistence (Sein und Zeit, 1927). Heidegger, who dealt with death ontologically, asserted that when a person faces his own death, his life becomes more purposeful. Death, moreover, being unique and personal, leads to a sense of individuality when we are conscious of it,

73

since no other person can die for us (cf.
Euripides, Alcestis). Each dies his own death.
Each dies alone! That is why ignoring death
obliterates our individuality. Besides, death
is more than the disintegration of a biological
system, and existence itself is understood
better when we also consider death. But we
cannot experience death, since this condition
is the cessation of experience. Heidegger
thus disarms death by incorporating it into
the consciousness. In brief, death becomes
the ultimate phenomenon of life as we search
for the meaning of existence.

Heidegger's ideas influenced Jean Paul
Sartre (born 1905), the French existentialist,
dramatist, novelist, and man of letters who
became a leader of the French Resistance during
World War II. His basic philosophical ideas
are as follows:

1. Essence is preceded by existence,
namely, man is the only creator of his ethics,
and God and absolute truth do not exist.

2. Man is unhappy, since he is alone and
free, having no Supreme Being above himself
to relate to.

3. Man must face his condition as
creatively as possible.

On the basis of this philosophy, Sartre
has said the following regarding death: the
self is finite, there is no immortal soul, the
end of life is followed by nonexistence, and
death is "the stranger." Moreover, constant
awareness of death intensifies the sense of
life, whereas ignoring death deprives life of
an element of urgency (Being and Nothingness,
1943; Existentialism as Humanism, 1946).

Finally, Albert Camus (1913-1960), the

74

French novelist, utilized the Greek myth of
Sisyphus in his philosophy. Sisyphus, who
built Corinth and became its first king, was
avaricious, cunning, and fraudulent: "where
Sisyphus lived, who was the craftiest of men"
(Homer, Iliad, VI, 153). When he revealed one
of Zeus's love affairs, the king of Olympus
sent Thanatos (Death) to punish Sisyphus, but
the clever king of Corinth succeeded in
throwing Thanatos into prison. When, later
on, he was finally near death, he deviously
instructed his wife, Merope, not to make the
usual funerary sacrifices to the gods. His
new trick was successful, since Persephone,
the queen of Hades, sent him back to the upper
world to reprimand his "faithless" wife! Old
age, however, for which there is no cure,
ultimately killed Sisyphus, who is now
punished forever in Hades as follows: "And
I saw Sisyphus suffering violently, supporting
a huge stone with both hands. Indeed, bracing
himself with hands and feet, he pushed the
stone toward the top of a hill; but when he
was about to move it over the summit, it would
heavily turn back; and down again to the plain
would roll the ruthless stone. Immediately,
he would strain again and push it back, and
the sweat flowed down from his limbs, and
dust rose up from his head" (Homer, Odyssey,
XI, 593-600). This tragic myth inspired
Camus to produce The Myth of Sisyphus in 1942.
After speculating about every major aspect of
life, death, and the universe, the French
novelist concluded that suicide is the only
true philosophical issue. He thus defined the
idea of the absurd, asserting that man finds
himself in a meaningless cosmos, and that
life's sole value derives from an understanding
of the conflict between man and what is not
man.

CHAPTER TWELVE

CONCLUSION

This book has dealt with the history and all important aspects of thanatology from primitive times to the present. A few of the main conclusions are as follows:

1. Despite the countless publications dealing with death, the end of life has not been defined satisfactorily as yet, and it seems that it will be a very long time before this is accomplished.

2. There is much disagreement among thinkers and systems concerning death in general.

3. Death is an exceedingly important philosophical, religious, social, psychological, legal, economic, and biological issue (Kathy Charmaz, The Social Reality of Death, 1980). We must neither ignore it nor overemphasize it morbidly, lugubriously, pathologically.

4. Thus, we must study every area of death objectively and systematically.

5. A very significant aspect is attitudes toward death. Construction of a Thanatometer (Death Measure), for instance, that is, a scientific instrument to measure human feelings and ideas regarding death, would supply us with a wealth of valuable data.

6. On the basis of these and other
relevant data, theoretical conclusions may
be drawn concerning the relationships
between death, on the one hand, and numerous
variables, on the other (age, gender, health,
race, education, occupation, income, family,
religion, ideology, and so forth).

7. Such findings may be employed
practically to help both the individual
and the group to solve various problems
associated with death.

8. Finally, for the present, the wisest
attitude toward life and death seems to be
what the author calls the Alcestis complex.
This concept consists of the following
elements:

a. Although the first written record of
Homo sapiens' discovery of death is 4,500
years old (in the Gilgamesh Epic of 2500 B.C.,
where King Gilgamesh speaks of death as
complete annihilation), we are still unable
to understand the very nature of death.

b. Similarly, even at the present time,
we lack truly convincing arguments concerning
the immortality of the soul. Serious
philosophical viewpoints are not entirely
acceptable: for instance, Henri Bergson's
emphasis on the independence of consciousness;
Max Scheler's analogous position; John
McTaggart's belief in the spirituality of all
existence and the continuity of the self
after death; Gabriel Marcel's acceptance of
the Socratic statement that "I am not my
body"; and William James's theory of the
"functional dependence" between soul and
brain. Much less convincing are the arguments
of "general consent" (universal belief in
immortality); spiritism; psychical research;
mystical evidence (Jacques Maritain's emphasis

on our "natural, instinctive knowledge" of
human immortality); and Goethe's assertion
that the end is inconceivable: "It is quite
impossible for a thinking being to imagine
nonbeing, a cessation of thought and life.
In this sense everyone carries the proof of
his own immortality within himself" (Johann
Peter Eckermann, Conversations with Goethe,
1852).

c. In view of such doubts, it seems
safer and nobler to lead a virtuous life
dominated by three ideals: knowledge, love,
and self-sacrifice. This type of life is
approximated by Alcestis, the wife of King
Admetus in the ancient city of Pherae. Thanks
to Apollo's intervention, Admetus would avoid
death if another person died in his stead.
Only the truly virtuous queen was willing to
die for her husband. His own father, selfish
old Pheres, merely protested, "I won't ask
you to die for me, and I won't die for you,"
which recalls the complaint of Achilles that
it is better to be a slave in the upper world
than a king among the ghastly phantoms of
Hades. Of course, the self-centered Admetus
was finally saved when he reached the heights
of virtue through his hospitable attitude
toward Hercules (Euripides, Alcestis). In
brief, in view of our limited knowledge of
the nature of life and death, the Alcestis
complex includes two elements, a virtuous life
and the willingness to sacrifice it on the
altar of the welfare of other human beings.

BIBLIOGRAPHY

Ariès, Philippe, Western Attitudes Toward
    Death: From the Middle Ages to the
    Present, Baltimore: Johns Hopkins
    University Press, 1974.
Ars Moriendi, Norwood, New Jersey: Jonson,
    1491 (1974).
Bailey, Lloyd, Biblical Perspectives on Death,
    Philadelphia: Fortress, 1978.
Bardis, Panos, "Counseling and the Evolution
    of the Concept of Sin," in Hirsch
    Silverman, editor, Marital Therapy,
    Springfield, Illinois: Thomas, 1972,
    pp. 178-209.
Becker, Ernest, The Denial of Death, New York:
    Macmillan, 1973.
Bendann, Effie, Death Customs, New York:
    Knopf, 1930.
Berrigan, Daniel, We Die Before We Live, New
    York: Seabury, 1980.
Bichat, Mari, Physiological Researches on
    Life and Death, New York: Arno, 1977.
Boase, Thomas, Death in the Middle Ages, New
    York: McGraw-Hill, 1972.
Carse, James, and Arlene Dallery, editors,
    Death and Society, New York: Harcourt
    Brace Jovanovich, 1977.
Choron, Jacques, Death and Western Thought,
    New York: Collier, 1963.
Crane, Diana, The Sanctity of Social Life, New
    York: Russell Sage, 1975.
Crichton, Ian, The Art of Dying, Atlantic
    Highlands, New Jersey: Humanities, 1976.
Dunne, John, The City of the Gods, New York:
    Macmillan, 1973.

81

Eccles, John, The Understanding of the Brain, New York: McGraw-Hill, 1973.

Edwards, Paul, editor, The Encyclopedia of Philosophy, New York: Macmillan, 1967.

Encyclopaedia Britannica, The New Encyclopaedia Britannica, 15th edition, Chicago: 1975.

Evans, W., The Chemistry of Death, Springfield, Illinois: Thomas, 1963.

Feifel, Herman, editor, The Meaning of Death, New York: McGraw-Hill, 1959.

Ferretti, Val, and David Scott, Death in Literature, New York: McGraw-Hill, 1977.

Flew, Antony, editor, Body, Mind, and Death, New York: Macmillan, 1964.

Frazer, James, The Belief in Immortality and the Worship of the Dead, London: Macmillan, 1913-1922.

Fulton, Robert, Death, Grief and Bereavement, New York: Arno Press, 1977.

Gatch, Milton, Death, New York: Seabury, 1969.

Glaser, Barney, and Anselm Strauss, Awareness of Dying, Chicago: Aldine, 1965.

Gorer, Geoffrey, Death, Grief, and Mourning, Garden City, New York: Doubleday, 1965.

Gruman, Gerald, A History of Ideas About the Prolongation of Life, New York: Arno, 1966.

Habenstein, Robert, and William Lamers, Funeral Customs the World Over, Milwaukee, Wisconsin: Bulfin, 1961.

Heidel, Alexander, Gilgamesh Epic and Old Testament Parallels, second edition, Chicago: University of Chicago Press, 1963.

Herbery, Will, Judaism and Modern Man, New York: Meridian, 1960.

Holck, Frederick, editor, Death and Eastern Thought, Nashville, Tennessee: Abingdon, 1974.

Hughes, Thomas, A Dictionary of Islam, Clifton, New Jersey: Reference Book Publishers, 1965.

Jung, Lee, Death and Beyond in the Eastern
    Perspective, new edition, New York:
    Gordon and Breach, 1974.
Kastenbaum, Robert, and Ruth Aisenberg, The
    Psychology of Death, New York: Springer,
    1972.
Kiernan, Thomas, Who's Who in the History of
    Philosophy, New York: Philosophical
    Library, 1965.
Kohl, Marvin, editor, Beneficent Euthanasia,
    Buffalo, New York: Prometheus, 1975.
Kübler-Ross, Elisabeth, On Death and Dying,
    New York: Macmillan, 1969.
Kutscher, Austin, and Austin Kutscher,
    A Bibliography of Books on Death,
    Bereavement, Loss and Grief, New York:
    Health Sciences Publishing Corp., 1969.
Langone, John, Death Is a Noun, Boston:
    Little Brown, 1972.
Lemaître, Solange, Le Mystère de la Mort Dans
    les Religions d'Asie, second edition:
    Paris: Maisonneuve, 1963.
Lifton, Robert, Broken Connection, New York:
    Simon and Schuster, 1979.
Lofland, Lyn, Toward a Sociology of Death and
    Dying, Beverly Hills, California: Sage,
    1976.
Maguire, Daniel, Death By Choice, Garden
    City, New York: Doubleday, 1974.
Meyers, David, The Human Body and the Law,
    Chicago: Aldine, 1970.
Mitford, Jessica, The American Way of Death,
    New York: Simon and Schuster, 1963.
O'Connor, Mary, The Art of Dying Well, New
    York: Columbia University Press, 1942.
Pardi, Marco, Death: An Anthropological
    Perspective, Washington: University
    Press of America, 1977.
Peterson, James, and Michael Briley, Widows
    and Widowhood, New York: Association
    Press, 1977.
Pike, Diane, Life Is Victorious! New York:
    Simon and Schuster, 1976.

Pincus, Lily, Death and the Family, New York: Random House, 1976.

Rahner, Karl, On the Theology of Death, New York: Herder and Herder, 1961.

Reich, Warren, editor, Encyclopedia of Bioethics, New York: Free Press, 1978.

Riemer, Jack, editor, Jewish Reflections on Death, New York: Schocken, 1974.

Schechter, Solomon, Some Aspects of Rabbinic Theology, New York: Macmillan, 1909.

Sills, David, editor, International Encyclopedia of the Social Sciences, New York: Macmillan, 1968.

Simpson, Michael, Dying, Death, and Grief, New York: Plenum, 1979.

Stendahl, Krister, editor, Immortality and Resurrection, New York: Macmillan, 1965.

Strugnell, Cecile, Adjustment to Widowhood and Some Related Problems, New York: Health Sciences, 1974.

Tromp, Nicholas, Primitive Conceptions of Death and the Nether World in the Old Testament, Rome: Pontifical Biblical Institute, 1969.

Tylor, Edward, Religion in Primitive Culture, London: Murray, 1871.

Veatch, Robert, Death, Dying, and the Biological Revolution, New Haven, Connecticut: Yale University Press, 1976.

Vermeule, Emily, Aspects of Death in Early Greek Art and Poetry, Berkeley, California: University of California Press, 1979.

Vernon, Glenn, Sociology of Death, New York: Ronald, 1972.

Warthin, Alfred, The Physician of the Dance of Death, New York: Arno, 1931 (1977).

Wass, Hannelore, et al., Death Education, Washington: Hemisphere, 1980.

Weir, Robert, editor, Death in Literature, New York: Columbia University Press, 1980.

INDEX

ABOUT THE AUTHOR
Panos D. Bardis

Born: Lefcohorion, Arcadia, Greece.
Education: Lyceum, Langadia, Greece;
Panteios Supreme School, Athens; Bethany
College, B.A., magna cum laude; Notre Dame
University, M.A.; Purdue University, Ph.D.

Teaching: Albion College and The
University of Toledo (currently Professor
of Sociology).

Organizations: American Association for
the Advancement of Science, Fellow; American
Sociological Association, Fellow; Conference
Internationale de Sociologie de la Religion;
Institut International de Sociologie, Fellow;
International Institute of Arts and Letters,
Geneva, Life Fellow; International
Sociological Association; World Academy of
Scholars, Fellow; World Poetry Society
Intercontinental; and about 40 others.

Editorships: Editor and Book Review
Editor, Social Science; Associate Editor of
22 other journals.

Who's Who: Contemporary Authors;
International Authors and Writers Who's Who;
Who's Who in America; Who's Who in the World;
World Who's Who in Science, 1700 B.C. -
1968 A.D.; and 40 others.

Publications: Many books (Ivan and
Artemis, a novel; History of the Family;
etc.); more than 200 articles (including first
English translation of Archimedes's lost work
"On Balances"); numerous poems ("Peleus and
Thetis"; "Usha"; "Aegean Dream"; etc.).

Musical compositions: 20 songs for
mandolin ("Byron Ballad"; "Jeu de Jason";
"Minerva Melody"; "The Pines of Olympia";
"Echoes of Arcadia"; etc.).

Travel: Throughout the world for
lectures and participation in international
scientific conferences.

Awards: Award for Outstanding Achievement
in Education; Outstanding Teaching Award.

91